In loving memory of
the Princess who never became queen
and Rowdy,
who would have been her consort

The Sphinxing Rabbit: Her Sovereign Majesty

First published in 2019 by

Panoma Press Ltd

48 St Vincent Drive, St Albans, Herts, AL1 5SJ, UK

info@panomapress.com

www.panomapress.com

Illustrations by Nilesh B. Mistry.

Book layout by Nilesh B. Mistry, Mainline Design Limited.

Printed in India

Printed on acid-free paper from managed forests.

ISBN 978-1-784521-54-7

The Sphinxing Rabbit

The story of the life regal and free

Written by Pauline Chakmakjian
Illustrated by Nilesh Mistry

The clever rabbit sat
under the Tree of Life.

One fruit fell from the tree and gave
The Sphinxing Rabbit special knowledge.

The Sphinxing Rabbit likes to visit similar insightful people in a far off land.

6

This place has its own way of doing things
with an etiquette bonus.
The Satoshis have their own domestic,
food-related, technological
and financial systems.

There are many cities throughout
the world with Masters.

For some time,
the biggest one has been this one.

This house has some sort of a master(s)
and several loyal dogs.

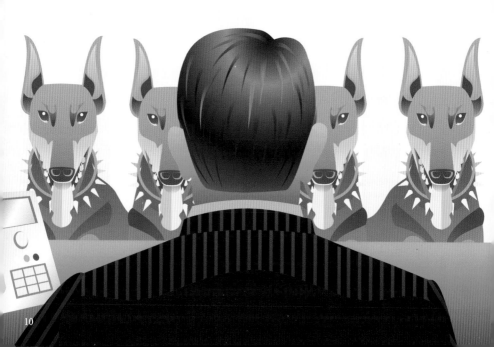

If they are not loyal,
they get beaten by a stick.

The Sphinxing Rabbit has no masters and has no slaves; she just wants to be left alone and have her own base of operations. She studied how each feudal lord built a section of Osaka Castle.

But, she needs military forces
in setting this up.

She must first get their attention
somehow, so she made a speech.

The bucks agreed to help
such an articulate beauty, of course!

Each buck dug out one section of the warren.

The Sphinxing Rabbit
oversees the work
of her allies
in a tranquil setting.

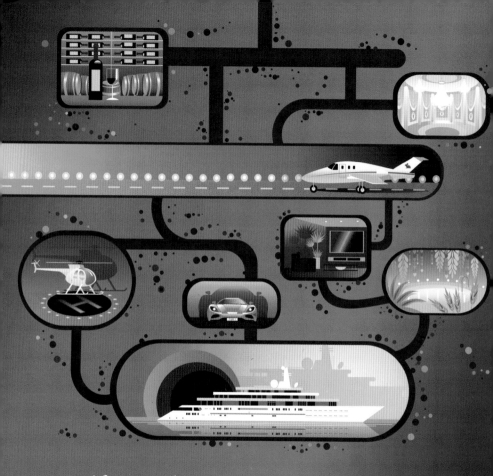

After several months, the warren is completed.

The bucks swear their loyalty to The Sphinxing Rabbit
and let her get on with things.

During the day, she sits by the entry of her base –
it rather looks as if she is doing nothing at all.

Drones pass by during the day
as part of surveillance.

Dusk is a very exciting time for
The Sphinxing Rabbit...

...because she can get to her business in private.

The next day, she just sits by
the entry to the warren again.

A few dogs watch The Sphinxing Rabbit
through their monitors.

"What does she do?"

One dog gets curious and goes to have a word with
The Sphinxing Rabbit.

There are cats about,
but they have independent lives.

The Sphinxing Rabbit: Good day, Sir.

Dog: Hello, what is your name?

The Sphinxing Rabbit: I am The Sphinxing Rabbit, what is yours?

Dog: I am Fido.

The Sphinxing Rabbit: How do you do, Fido?

Dog: What do you do?

The Sphinxing Rabbit: Nothing much, I like to rest, watch and be quiet with my thoughts. What is it that you do?

Dog: I serve my master without thought.

The Sphinxing Rabbit: Oh, how very interesting.

Dog: Don't you have a master?

The Sphinxing Rabbit: No, don't be ridiculous.

Dog: Do you have slaves?

The Sphinxing Rabbit: No.

Dog: So, you just sit here all day?

The Sphinxing Rabbit: Yes, something like that.

Bewildered, the dog then left.

The Sphinxing Rabbit responded to carrots
found here and there in every form.

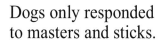

Dogs only responded
to masters and sticks.

The dogs meet and express
thoughts about
The Sphinxing Rabbit.

They report the suspicious rabbit
to their Master.

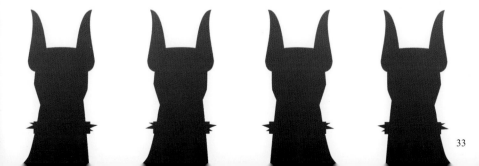

Meanwhile, The Sphinxing Rabbit
goes into the warren for an
overnight trip in
her private jet.

The Sphinxing Rabbit likes
to visit Hawai'i at times.

The Dog House decided to
send a Ladybug to spy on
The Sphinxing Rabbit.

The Ladybug is given a small incentive.

The Sphinxing Rabbit had returned from holiday
when the Ladybug approached her.

"You seem cozy... May I befriend you?"

The Sphinxing Rabbit trusted the Ladybug and invited it
inside (one section of the warren only)
for hospitality and entertainments.

The Ladybug liked the atmosphere of
The Sphinxing Rabbit's lifestyle.
In fact, it preferred it.

The Ladybug told The Sphinxing Rabbit everything
and they became close friends.
They used the bribe money to buy a time machine
to travel to more interesting moments.

They would go to fun places
through the time portal.

Like the chateau of Madame Budgie Dots
for fancy feasts and lavish parties
and excellent conversations.

Back at the Dog House, the Master and his loyal servants
thought of ways to disturb the peace and joy
of The Sphinxing Rabbit and her little companion.

They decide to send an insect drone like the Ladybug
to spy on The Sphinxing Rabbit.

The Ladybot slowly approached The Sphinxing Rabbit and the Ladybug, both resting as usual.

The Ladybot expressed a desire to get to know them.

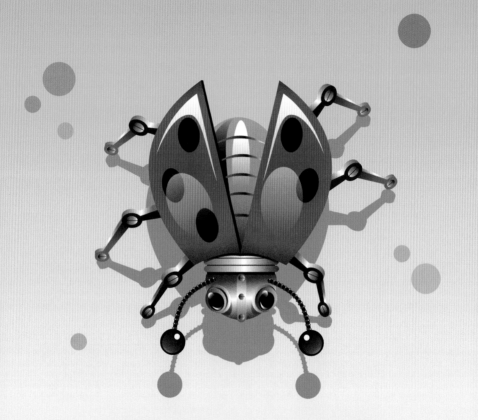

The Sphinxing Rabbit noticed something -
one dot was missing from this Ladybug.

The Sphinxing Rabbit invited the Ladybot for
hospitality inside the warren,
but said it had to be hoodwinked
for privacy purposes.

They took the Ladybot into a chamber in the warren that shuts down mechanical objects.

The dogs were worried when
their monitors went blank.

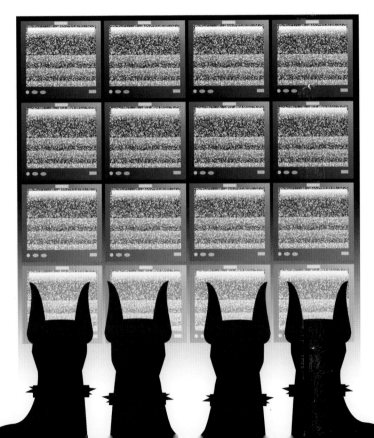

The Sphinxing Rabbit then placed
a disinformation program inside the Ladybot.

When the Ladybot was turned back on,
the dogs thought it was just a glitch and could see
what was inside the warren of The Sphinxing Rabbit.

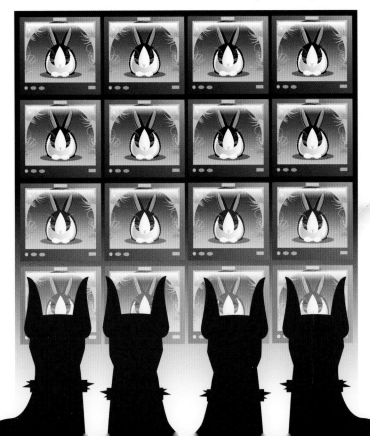

The dogs reported to their Master that
The Sphinxing Rabbit was no threat at all.

The dogs then went after a showy,
loud peacock instead.

And so, The Sphinxing Rabbit and the Ladybug
were at rest once again.

The next evening, The Sphinxing Rabbit performed
a military inspection of her weapons in the warren
in preparation for any warfare for defensive purposes.

To be continued...

Special thanks to

David Turner,
Alderman Professor Michael Mainelli
and my father, Dr. George Chakmakjian

Author

Pauline Chakmakjian is an author,
artist, public speaker, advisor
and a Visit Kyoto Ambassador.

Illustrator

Nilesh Mistry is an illustrator,
designer and mural artist.
www.nileshmistryart.com